Love the Real You

Love the Real You

Publisher: Pen Legacy Publishing

www.penlegacy.com

Love the Real You written by: Charron Monaye
Cover Graphics by: Junnita Jackson
Editing Services by: Summer Willow Fitch
Insight coaching: Vaughn McNeill & Dr. Syleecia Thompson
Photographer, Hair & Makeup for Charron Monaye done by: Brenda Lee

LOVE THE REAL YOU.

Copyright © 2015 by Charron Monaye.

All rights reserved. Printed in the United States of America. No part of this book may be used or reproduced in any manner whatsoever without permission except in the case of brief quotations embodied in critical articles or reviews.

Pen Legacy books may be purchased for educational, business, or sales promotional use. For information please e-mail the special Markets Department at lovetherealyou0510@gmail.com.

First Edition
Library of Congress Catalog-2015938537
Paperback ISBN: 978-0-9961880-0-5
E-Book ISBN: 978-0-9961880-1-2

This book is dedicated to the one who was patient, kind and understanding enough to help me to finally recognize who I really am.
Thank you!!

*Reminder: the only things guaranteed in life are your birth date and a date of death.
However the 'dash' in-between is up to you!
What you do with your life is truly your choice. This book is geared to assist, motivate and encourage you to achieve greatness at the highest benefit of yourself.
- Charron Monaye*

Contents

Introduction

Foreword

The Power of Love

Declare Who You Are
- Your "Divine Assignment" is Calling You
- The Blueprint was Already Written
- Are You Living Your Dreams
- You Are Perfectly Imperfect

Stop Playing the Blame Game
- Parents
- Relationships
- Failures

I Deserve Better
- Cost Benefit
- The Only Validation You Require Is Your Own

Love the Real you Purposely
- Know Your Worth
- It's Time to Transform Your Mindset
- Be Comfortable with Yourself

The Power in Finances
- Money Doesn't Make you - You Make Money
- Financing Your Purpose

In the Midst of Living, Never Forget to Love Yourself

- Moving Forward
- I Finally Love Me

Introduction
Are you Ready to **Do the Work!**

Let me thank you for taking the first step in becoming a better you for **YOU**! We live in a society where some people live to take from, feed off of or depend solely on others for personal gain. It's almost like it's easier for some to live vicariously through you and *your* accomplishments instead of doing their own work. It hurts to think that there are more leeches than friends, more hidden agendas than honesty and more backbiters than people who are loyal. However, you have the right to live, love and laugh without the permission of another. When you discover the power of love and respect for yourself, you will no longer allow others to disrespect or discredit your hard work and happiness.

You may ask yourself, "How can I learn who I really am when I have to wear so many hats for others? I am a caregiver, leader in an organization and employee - I have very little time for myself". You are not alone. Many are forced to run households, care for parents, be a loving husband/wife or productive employee and by the time they are finished being everything for everyone all they want to do is sleep. There are not enough hours in a day, week or a year for us to fully learn our true selves. We become so programmed by everyday happenings in life that we can sometimes forget our own names. This is not living and this is not how you should practice loving yourself. At this point in your life, aren't you tired of:

- *Working only to pay bills*
- *Running for everyone with no one seeming to reciprocate*
- *Beating yourself up for making unproductive choices*

How can you effectively love and care for anyone if your burning the candle at both ends? You cannot continue to live for the betterment of others, a job, friends, lovers or your family at the expense of hindering your own growth and happiness. That's why today, I am challenging you to take the first step to cleansing and renewing your mindset in order to *Love the Real You* - on purpose. This was the challenge that led me to write this book, *Love the Real You*. This book began as a journal entry where I simply used my pen to release everything that was holding me back from purposefully walking in my destiny. I was not living the life that I wanted and it was in the moment of me hitting "rock bottom" where I discovered the need to release and forgive; while finding the strength to rebuild and rebirth a much stronger, wiser and healthier version of me.

Writing this book, also, allowed me to become my own personal life coach. I had to finally address my past, face my hindrances, acknowledge my fears and accept my choices without blaming others. I had to find the right answers and move in the right direction. This journal entry became *my* coaching tool and I decided to use it to inspire others who know that their current situations are "not all that life had to offer". It's always great to go to others for advice, join networks for motivation and seek refuge from a spiritual being, but through my transformation journey I learned that the answers to my problems lie within me- *the real me*. I was ready to do the work! It was pointless to pay a therapist, a life coach or even run to my pastor for rescue because the only person who could save me from my destruction was me – it was my choice.

Acknowledging true *Love*, *Respect* and *Desires of your heart* brings forth understanding and will heal your broken spirit. Are you ready to transform? Are you excited about letting go of your past? Most importantly, are you ready to be introduced to your truest self all over again? If you answered yes, to all of those questions, then it's time to get to work. I must warn you, if you are looking for me to answer your questions, teach you how to be a better you and tell you my life story so you can compare my flaws to yours, then this book is not for you. I cannot teach you who you are nor can I tell you what purpose or choice is good for you. I can however, provide you with information, challenge you to think about your past and offer my experience as a guide to give you alternative methods. In order for this book to be effective, I need you to commit 100% of yourself. Understand that my challenges come from a place of love. Be open-minded to changing your perspective and remain honest as you complete the "Coaching Corner Questions". My coaching principles will allow you to see your purpose and your direction in black and white. These principles will also provide a visual pulse check to gauge progress and offer immediate encouragement as you transition to more substantive expressions of self-love.

Since we know there is more to life than what we currently have or see; it is time to put on our coaching hats and embark on this journey together. Let's go to work!!

Foreword
Let's take a walk down memory lane

It was 1997; a beautiful and crisp day in April at West Chester University. The campus was buzzing because spring was not the only thing that had just arrived. Four of my best friends and I had just become members of Zeta Phi Beta Sorority, Inc. – we were elated and our first step show was one of the most anticipated events of the semester. There were many who came to support our coming out party. I remember like it was yesterday; cheering, cameras flashing and the sound of stomping feet on the gym floor. Behind one of those cameras was Charron Monaye; she was a friend who was always so supportive of the sorority's efforts on and off campus. I surely was not surprised when she also became a member of Zeta Phi Beta Sorority, Inc. in the fall of 2005. Little did we know – being Zetas wasn't the only thing we would have in common. Much greater things were on the horizon for our sisterhood.

My first introduction to Charron Monaye's talent as a writer was through song. I had no idea that she was such a thoughtful poet and song writer until she asked me for a favor in 2008. This was the pivotal moment where we discovered our shared penchant for the arts - particularly music and creative writing. She said she had an arsenal of songs that she was preparing to get placed and needed me to vocally produce and perform her demo submissions. I knew she wrote poetry and songs but I had never had the pleasure of experiencing them- I was a fan instantly. I could tell from her writing that she had experienced pain in her relationships but her songs were riddled with strength. Her lyrics were raw emotions that she transformed into words. Even though she could not sing a lick [truth] I became her melodic translator and it was easy because I could really feel what she had written. I recorded a few songs for her but then- she disappeared.

After a few years, Charron resurfaced on the social media scene in pictures with some of the biggest names in the music industry, big name playwrights and up and coming talent. I was so proud. When we finally got a chance to catch up and discuss what had transpired over the years; we discovered that we had similar stories. We both had been going through raging storms in our personal lives. We were fighting to find our places in the entertainment industry, our relationships and in our careers. We were both *desperately* fighting to regain our passion. What was our mission? Why were we so afraid to succeed when we truly believed in our talents?

After trading stories we both realized that in hindsight our pain bought us to places where our only choice was to reconnect with passion and live our lives on purpose. Charron went full throttle with her writing and wrote several successful plays and *at that time,* two books. My soul hit rock bottom and I was so fed up with allowing my relationship failures to capsize my dreams that I finally decided to focus all my energy on my goals and do what I *knew* was right. I resurrected my mixology services and instruction by launching Summerwillow.com. I started a love/relationship coaching forum through my *Hearts & Hangovers Blog and* with personal clientele. Currently I am putting the finishing touches on my first book *Let Me Tell You Like I Told Myself;* a guide to assist with finding, trusting and following your truth in love.

Love the Real You

Charron and I realized that as we fought tirelessly through failure and uncertainty we were transformed *through* the journey to becoming stronger. We were finally ready and willing to share what we learned in our darkest hours. The sting of experiencing mindless repeats of the wrong scenarios drove us to find the best solutions for happy and purposeful living. My first book was already in process when Charron asked me to write the foreword for her third book, *Love the Real You*; and her book is a wonderful tool that reminds me to continue to break the chains of fear, doubt and failure and to regain and retain my power.

Do you want to understand your mission in life? Do you want to find out what is holding you back from living passionately on purpose? We all know what we don't want but do you want to discover what you do want? It is never too late. *Love the Real You* places emphasis on stopping the blame game and teaches you how to embrace your mistakes. Learn how to lean on your own thoughts and desires and to steer clear of the need for validation. *Love the Real You* takes you on a step by step journey to rededicate yourself to your purpose; empowering you to be excited about who you are *within*. Revisit your old habits, attitudes and reasons why you have not harnessed your power. Get your pen and let down your guard; your honesty will free you and this book is your guide. Are you ready?

Summer Willow Fitch
contact@summerwillow.com
www.summerwillow.com
www.girltinilive.com/tag/heartsandhangovers
Philadelphia, PA
April 2015

The Power of Love

In 1 Corinthians 13:4-7 love is defined this way: "Love is patient, love is kind. It does not envy, it does not boast, it is not proud. It does not dishonor others, it is not self-seeking, it is not easily angered and it keeps no record of wrongs. Love does not delight in evil but rejoices with the truth. It always protects, always trusts, always hopes and always perseveres."

When you naturally love who you are and all the good things about you, you can openly embrace your life's possibilities. By not recognizing the good qualities you possess; you may allow others to alter your attitudes and seemingly recreate your possibilities. As you read each chapter and begin to identify your fears, hindrances and the state of your emotions, you will eventually see that the common denominator is how you love yourself. Therefore, we must revitalize your power and rekindle your love for self before you can extend any support or love to anyone else.

I will love myself by

_____

_____

_____

_____

_____

_____

_____

When you take the time to love yourself, these four things will seem to happen almost instantly:

- **You accept who you are** ~ When you accept who you are, you feel no need to be counterfeit or compare yourself to others.
- **You will avoid self-reproach** ~ Self-reproach, sorrow and a sense of shame can be difficult to experience.
- **You look better** ~ When you accept your perfect imperfections you will become more aware of how beautiful you really are.
- **The world around you changes** ~ Falling in love with yourself enables you to look at things, people and life from another perspective - a better perspective.

Self-love makes you feel good about who you are and the world has no choice other than to reflect that love.

Chapter 1
Declare Who You Are

Coaching Corner

Before you embark on this chapter, ponder these questions. Be prepared to answer them as you read each section:

What is my divine assignment?
When I was growing up, what did I dream of becoming?
Am I that person now?
Am I living in my purpose and enjoying my passion?
Why am I so intrigued with being perfect?

Your "Divine Assignment" is Calling You

If someone walked up to you and asked, "Who are you?" what would you say? Would your answer reflect your occupation or your passion? What defines you? When choosing your education or career do you decide based upon passion or paycheck? One may choose to be a doctor over a singer because the paycheck may be more appealing. However, that same person may only find happiness when on the stage (hmmm). So what defines your happiness? When doing for others does *their* happiness trump *your* happiness? Sure you want your siblings and parents to feel loved and appreciated - but would this be at the expense of your time and resources? It is sometimes difficult to find a balance between doing what's best for others versus yourself. For example, I have a friend who has a job where she is really unhappy. She also, has the obligation to care for her sick grandmother. Because of this obligation, she has stopped living her life and pursuing her dreams so that she can provide for her grandmother's well-being. This friend has pretty much given up on life and spends her days complaining when she *actually* has the ability to change her circumstances. Instead of being frustrated with her, I realized that she is no longer in tune with her passion is. She can no longer connect to the things that make her happy because she thinks her sole purpose is to be a caregiver - and that's not true. Some of us go through life never being able to define our purpose or allow life to take us off track. If this goes on for too long, we may lose our passion for life and forget the desires of our hearts. We sometimes lose sight of our passionate connection to living. We must revisit and rediscover the true meaning of our existence. To do this let's examine a few things that may be taking you off track. Are you:

- *People pleasing*
- *Seeking validation from others*
- *Finding people to make you happy*
- *Working in an unfulfilling job*
- *Living someone else's vision*

Feeling the need to do any of the above mentioned things is a sign that you are not living in your purpose. Your purpose is something that motivates you to become the best version of yourself as you journey through life. In addition, it is something that connects you to your calling or your "Divine Assignment". Knowing your divine assignment is an important key to living a rewarding and successful life. Your "divine assignment" defines your true passion and links you to your purpose. Your purpose is defined as, "the reason for which something is done or created or for which something exists." and your passion is defined as, "a strong desire for something." Understanding their differences is required to help you travel down the *right* path.

What is my Personal Desire? (Passion)

_____
_____
_____
_____
_____

Why was I Created? (Purpose)

_____
_____
_____
_____
_____

Answering these questions will make understanding your purpose clearer. When I was 12 years old, I performed one of my poems entitled "Alone" at the United Negro College Fund Telethon banquet. I was always writing poems but this opportunity solidified my passion for writing. But it wasn't until my early 30's that I realized my purpose in life was to inspire people to own and live in *their* purpose. So now, I can define who I am by saying, ***"Charron Monaye is a person who loves to educate, inspire and elevate people to walk in their own destiny while using her gift of writing to fulfill and motivate herself and others to keep striving to find their voices"***. During the 30 year process to find and define who I was, I experienced many "seasons". I experienced unhealthy circumstances that taught me what I could no longer accept. These dark seasons hurt me and unfortunately interfered with my divine purpose. But the fruitful seasons returned and I realized that I had to remain steadfast in knowing who I was no matter what I was going through. I had to know who I was and remind myself when life got rough. Now if you can, define who you are so you can remind yourself later.

Who are you?

_____

_____

_____

_____

_____

Lady Gaga once said, "Don't you ever let a soul in the world tell you that you can't be exactly who you are." You will never advance in life living for someone else's purpose. Not knowing who I was allowed people to redefine me for their own benefit. I am not argumentative and I can be extremely sensitive- so people sometime use that to their advantage. Some used anger, arguments and pressure as a means to get me to cave in to their demands. Even though I didn't want to do half the stuff I took on, I did it anyway. I felt like standing up for myself would have taken me out of character and walking away would have burned a bridge between us. Since I was all about pleasing others, I abandoned my dignity and self-love just so people could walk away fulfilled. I had to ask myself, "How was that helping me"? It wasn't. Therefore, I had to make a decision- them or me. Once I did the work and made the choices, I found my real purpose and passion. The deterrent train no longer stops at my station.

I hope that you are living in your purpose and not living in someone else's confusion. You are so deserving of the life you envisioned regardless of what others think or say.

Some of the things you can do to help toward your purpose are;
- **Learn about you** ~ When you know what makes you happy you'll be able to purge the behaviors that don't work for you.
- **Experience life** ~ Trying new things will help you think outside the box and get you to see the world outside of the bubble that you've allowed people to put you in.
- **Go back to school** ~ Research a major or a skill certification that you truly love and become knowledgeable in it. When you enhance your knowledge, you strengthen your ability to achieve success.
- **Love yourself** ~ When you love yourself, embrace your flaws and accept your gifts it becomes harder for others to recreate you.

Your purpose is your passport.
You must know where you are going in order to arrive there.

The Blueprint was Already Written

Jeremiah 29:11 says, "For I know the plans I have for you, declares the Lord, plans for welfare and not for evil, to give you a future and a hope."

Now that you have defined your purpose, passion and who you are, it's time to write out your mission in order to possess a visual to commit to during your transformation journey. At this time, I want you to think of yourself as a business and brand.

- *If you had to sell yourself to someone what would your 2-minute elevator pitch be?*
- *How would you market yourself?*
- *If you could put a price tag on your abilities and qualifications, how much would your product or service cost?*

I know that thinking of yourself as a business may seem foreign, but implementing the steps to start a business (planning, visioning and strategizing) in your life will begin to show you that certain steps are relevant to understanding your mission. For example, if you find that your passion is to be an actor, I will tell you that the line for successful Hollywood careers is quite long and extremely competitive but you can do it. So while you gain experience booking roles on and off Broadway, you need to remain abreast of the industry by attending workshops, networking with casting directors and possibly learning from a mentor. As you learn your skill and connect with others in the industry – determine what sets *you* apart. This industry is competitive. It seems that the easiest way to land a role is by exemplifying the skill sets that sets you apart and best fits with the needs of the casting director. Your ability to stand out will catch the right people's attention and land you the role. Following me now? Great!

According to Entrepreneur.com, "A mission statement defines what an organization is, why it exists and its reason for being" which is the same thing we are trying to build on here. Completing a mission statement will provide a concrete visual of what your journey should look like and the work necessary to get to your destination. The first part of your statement is identifying your purpose which we already completed, so I would like for you to take a few minutes to restate that below:

_____
_____
_____
_____
_____
_____
_____

Okay, now let's examine what your greatest attributes are and how you can offer them to benefit yourself and others. Depending on what your purpose and passion is, you may need to foster relationships to help you achieve your dreams – otherwise known as networking. Here is a little secret that I have learned being a writer in the music/theater/literary industries; Execs are not only interested in your talents they want to know that you are a total package. They want to know **what you have to offer.** You are not the only one with a purpose or passion, so the easiest way to decide who lands the opportunity is by determining who offers the best package. Think about what sets you apart and what you have to offer and write it.

1. _____
2. _____
3. _____
4. _____

Now, let's decide how to implement this mission and remain committed. Commitment is by far one of the hardest things you will do when it comes to this transformation journey. As soon as you begin your journey, you will be tested by naysayers, financial snafus, lack of support, etc. However, with all that could go wrong; staying focused, remaining flexible and not accepting "No" as "Never" will be the difference between success and failure. So as we finish the mission, I would like for you to start speaking your commitment and dedication into existence. Do not allow outside forces to sidetrack your life plans. Think about ways you can be **committed to your purpose** and write them below.

1. _____
2. _____
3. _____

4. _____
   _____

Excellent, so now let's put this mission statement together. Take your purpose, what you have to offer and ways to be committed and condense them into a statement that you can use as a guide to stay on track. Write your completed mission statement below.

_____
_____
_____
_____
_____
_____
_____

   Now that you have written out your mission statement, it's time to network and bring things to fruition. You now have the tools to birth your purpose, how will you proceed? Are you comfortable with the work you just completed? Did you get the answers you expected? When you can answer the "WHY", "HOW", "WHO", "WHAT" to your journey, the "WHEN" will come when you least expect it. Start preparing now.

   Before you are granted anything in life, you must first be tested to ensure that you are prepared to receive it. As my Christian friends would always remind me, "God will never put more on you than you can bear." Even though the test may weaken your spirit and challenge your mindset, don't doubt your abilities and you will see just how strong and how much of a survivor you are.

You never know just how strong you are until walking in your purpose and pursuing your life unapologetically is *your choice*.

Are you living your dreams?

As children we envision ourselves becoming doctors, teachers, police officers and lawyers. We envisioned our favorite car by playing the game, "That's my Car". We watched television and pictured our homes to look like the ones we saw on MTV cribs or other reality shows. We looked at entertainers and leading ladies imagining how we wanted our husbands and wives to look. I swear, by the age of 10, we had our entire lives planned but did we ever execute our dreams? Before we move forward, I want you to think back on all of your dreams and list what you envisioned for your life.

What were your Dreams?

What kind of car did you want to drive:

_____
_____
_____
_____

What kind of house did you want to live in:

_____
_____
_____
_____

What was your dream profession:

_____
_____
_____
_____

What did you want your husband/wife to be like:

_____
_____
_____
_____

When you look at this list, how does it make you feel? When you observe your current reality are you satisfied with your decisions or do you regret the paths you've taken? Look at your life currently and list your reality.

What is your Reality?

What kind of car do you drive:

_____
_____
_____
_____

What kind of house do you live in:

_____
_____
_____
_____

What is your profession:

_____
_____
_____
_____

Is your husband/wife all you dreamed they would be:

_____
_____
_____
_____

Did any of your dreams come to fruition? If so, that's great and I will be the first to applaud you. Unfortunately, many people will do this assignment and find that they haven't accomplished many of the dreams they've envisioned. Some may have a house, but it's not their dream house.

Some have a job but not their dream profession. A few may have a husband/wife but are they the mates of their dreams? Many of us are not living out our dreams and we need to look inside to discover why. Did you do everything within your power to align yourself with your dreams? Did you settle for what came easy instead of waiting for what felt right? We cannot expect for our dreams to come true if we are not determined to sacrifice and risk it all in order to achieve greatness. Are you comfortable with your reality or are you ready to achieve your dream life?

In order to bridge the gap, you have to look within and determine what stopped you. Did you stand in your own way preventing yourself from succeeding or did you allow others to persuade you that your dreams are unrealistic? No matter how you answer the questions, we need to find a way to inspire you to bring those dreams into reality. However, before we can move anything into the present, we need to eliminate those plaguing attitudes that delayed your progress. Addressing them now will prevent them from recurring.

My hindrances in life were?

_____
_____
_____
_____
_____
_____
_____

If you noticed, I asked what "were" your hindrances because, as of today, they are a thing of the past. I am encouraging you not to rehash them ever again. This journey is not designed for you to maintain the same mindset but to transform your thoughts. Your past delays are now stepping stones. So now, what will you do to make your dreams come true within the next 10 years?

What will I do to achieve my dreams now?

_____
_____
_____
_____
_____
_____
_____
_____
_____

You are Perfectly Imperfect
_____

I don't understand what it is about the word "perfect" that drives some people to drinking, drugs, and/or to committing suicide. Perfection is a status that some seem to strive for knowing they will fail. Will anyone ever be 100% perfect? Tell the word "perfect" means to you.

_____
_____
_____
_____
_____

According to the Merriam – Webster Dictionary the word **perfect** is defined as, "being entirely without fault or defect; completely correct or accurate; lacking in no essential detail". We sometime use synonyms of being flawless, impeccable and unblemished. I have yet to meet anyone or anything that matches this definition or these synonyms. Let's look up **human**; this is defined as "having good or bad qualities that people usually have". So if human is defined as having good or bad qualities but perfect is being flawless or unblemished, how can we expect humans to be something that by nature they will never be? Let's decide now that you are no longer going to strive for becoming perfect. Stop beating yourself up and learn how to embrace being perfectly imperfect. I often say, "I love my imperfections so much that I no longer care how flawed I am".

Like most people, I used to allow the term "perfect" to dictate who I was or was not. I stopped living my dreams and discovering my passion because it wasn't perfect to the masses. I would bash myself so much that hearing it from others wouldn't bother me. Have you ever talked down on yourself so much that people would just look at you and cry out of pity? My self-esteem fell so low because I felt inadequate and often regret my love of writing. Some people will rip the life right out of your soul because your version of perfect does not equate to theirs. If you are not careful some will break your spirit to the point of vulnerability so that they can rebuild you into their idea of what perfect is. I have been writing since I was 10 years old and for years it was the center of arguments because it conflicted with who others wanted me to be. In some cases, I persuaded myself to give up writing just so I could try and be "the perfect one" but that left me feeling miserable and voiceless. Living a life where you have no control over yourself is a horror that I would never wish for another to have to endure.

Instead of changing to be accepted, accept who you are and embrace the love within. The late great Dr. Maya Angelou wrote a phrase in her book, "Letter to My Daughter", that says, "You may not control all the events that happen to you, but you can decide not to be reduced by them." Don't run from your imperfections- learn from them. I guarantee you it will save you a lot of headaches later. Most importantly, stop giving people power! No one should be able to come into your space and dictate what your perfection should look like. If you like it, they should love it and if not, they can "exit stage left" (as we say in theater). I once had a man tell me, "you may not be perfect but you are perfect for me" and I could do nothing more than smile because it gave me inspiration to believe the same. It was at that point where I simply stopped trying to re-adjust my life trying to be perfect for someone else. I owed it to myself to be the person who God created – the one that my mother loves, my children respect and ultimately who I am proud of. This is your life and your story so live it being who you are, unapologetically. If someone appreciates your flaws they are worth your time, but if you have to change to fit in, don't waste your time. Always remember, your imperfections are minor setbacks, but will be the set up for your comeback.

Transformation Zone

Name three ways you are going to implement living in your Divine Assignment:

1. _____
   _____

2. _____

3. _____

Affirmation

I am the architect of my life; I build the foundation and choose its contents.

Chapter 2
Stop Playing the Blame Game

Coaching Corner

Before you embark on this chapter, ponder these questions and be prepared to answer them as you read each section.

Am I currently holding a grudge against my parents for who I am?
Are my failed relationships hindering my ability to create positive ones?
What role did I play in my failures? What did I learn from it?
Can I forgive others and myself in order to move on?

Parents

So often I hear people say, "If it wasn't for my dad leaving me when I was younger I would not be in this situation" or "If I had a mother who loved me more than she loved her man, I would be a more loving parent to my children." Although I understand how some can have these feelings at some point in life we need to let that go and use their mistakes as building blocks to enhance ourselves. Yes, they were supposed to:

- *Be the first teachers*
- *Provide us with the basic necessities to survive*
- *Prepare us to be productive citizens*
- *Love us because we were not asked to be here*
- *Give us their very best*

But, many of us fail to understand that our parents were not given an instruction manual and they are humans who made and will continue to make mistakes. They gave you what they could and you are responsible to make the best of it. I am not saying that all parents are angels and/or right in their style of parenting, but what I am saying is you should not punish anyone for your parent's errors. Their choices may have made life harder for you, but what are you doing now to do better? You deserve it all and don't have to remain stagnate because of how you may have been raised. Whatever your parents did not provide you with; you now have the choice to provide it for yourself. Life might have started with your parents, but it does not have to always end with them. What are you doing to change your mindset, gain new skills or feel better about yourself? I know it's hard to let go of what you had to endure because you were not asked to be here but neither were your parents. At some point, we must stop using the blame game as a way to justify our choices. When do you start taking responsibility and accountability for your own actions and owning your life? Being accountable for your own choices fosters growth, maturity and the ability to look for solutions when there's a problem.

For example, I spent the last 7 years of my childhood living in North Philadelphia where some of my friends lived with some of the craziest family dynamics. While attending school; some had to work part time jobs, others had to work the corners and a few had to drop out of school. But when I look at those same friends almost 20 years later, I see that the ones who had the most difficult situations went on to become politicians, officers in the U.S. Armed Forces, doctors and hold other high profile positions. They did not allow their past situations to destroy their future. So if they can do it, you can too. All you need is determination, self-motivation and the desire for more. Your parent's love or lack thereof does not have to be the blueprint of your life. You have the key to rewrite your story. I would like for you to go back to your childhood; identify every grudge, heartbreak and incident that has affected your journey. These past struggles are the culprit for your recent failures. You can't continue to hold on to things that don't serve you any purpose. You will never forget what happened to you, but you have to learn to let go and heal so that you can walk freely. In order to accomplish this, I would like for you to write a note to your Mother and Father and release them from the past and the affects it had on your life. Today allow your words to speak to their hearts with love.

Dear Mother,

Dear Father,

_____
_____
_____
_____
_____
_____
_____

Now, I want you to insert their names below and repeat;
_____ and
_____, I forgive you!

When I went away to college and started surrounding myself with members of the National Pan-Hellenic Council, I often heard the members recite "Excuses" which said, ***"Excuses are tools of the weak and incompetent, which create monuments of nothingness and those who specialize in them are seldom capable of anything else."*** (Author Unknown) I thought it was something that only members could recite, but as I matured I found new meaning and respect for this saying. We will never get anywhere in life by making excuses about why we are not where we want to be or believing that what our parents did hindered our potential. We decide our fate.

Today is a new day and your time is now to fully eliminate the excuses, forgive your parents and take accountability for your life.

Relationships

Understanding the power of relationships is essential to your growth and purpose. As I stated prior, depending upon your purpose and passion, it *may be crucial* to interact and build positive relationships. Whether, professional or personal, how you build relationships can benefit or be the demise of your livelihood. To this point, your relationships should be monitored and sometimes reevaluated in order to receive the maximum reward.

Working Relationships

When we think about the term "working relationships" consider co-workers or individuals who are connected to the pursuit of your dreams and financial stability. They are people who are there to teach, motivate and mentor us as we climb the ladder to success. You may be blessed to build relationships with people who genuinely invested in your future. These working relationships will grow your industry knowledge, link you to other professionals and give you an overall sense of confidence. In contrast, have you ever gotten close to a co-worker that you considered to be a friend, only to find out they were spreading your business around the office? Or have you had a business partner who used your knowledge to gain profits from your efforts? Being betrayed by a person who you thought had your back professionally is damaging and difficult to overcome.

For those who have built positive working relationship, it may be easy for you to continue to build your network, but if you have been wronged, holding on to a negative idea of building working relationship will not benefit your purpose. If you had a vision of being an actor but was burnt by casting directors in the past, you can't blame them for your lack of success. So what are you going to do; look back 15 years and say I could be Hollywood actor but I got duped? No! You were not duped. You stopped acting. You do not lose your gift/passion if someone does you wrong - you must keep striving. It's not someone else's fault, it your choice. It didn't feel good to be wronged, it never does, but you have to dust yourself off, forgive and move on with your life. Forgive those who have stolen your ideas, robbed you of your vision or bankrupt your journey. Forgive what could have been bad judgment on your part and encourage yourself to leap forward to new partnerships. *Next time you will know what to look for.* At this time, I would like for you to think about your previous working relationships. How they have shaped and affected your journey? If necessary, use your answers to heal.

Have working relationships positively/negatively affected your attitude? Explain.

_____
_____
_____
_____
_____

What have you achieved/not achieve because of this?

_____
_____
_____

Consider these attributes as you develop and mature new ones:

- **Identify your relationship needs** ~ Understand what you need from others and what they need from you.
- **Focus and develop your emotional intelligence** ~ Spend time developing and recognizing your emotions and what they are telling you.
- **Be positive** ~ Positivity strengthens relationships.
- **Maintain your boundaries** ~ Know how much time you can devote during the work day for social interactions.
- **Avoid gossip** ~ Gossiping will exacerbate situations and will cause mistrust and animosity between you and others.
- **Mutual respect** ~ When you respect the people that you work with, you value their input and ideas and they value yours.

Working relationships are essential to the success of your journey; whether in the confines of Corporate America or in the entrepreneurial ream, here are a few tips to maintain healthy working relationships:

- *Understand your mission*
- *Align yourself with like-minded people*
- *Keep the lines of communication open*

Examining intent is the key when hiring a partner, befriending a co-worker or creating a business team.

Intimate Relationships

Love is a beautiful thing! When you come into your purpose and you are pursuing your passion you want to have someone special in your life that is supportive. After a long day working towards your goal it's important to come home to someone who can understand and encourage you to fight another day. This person is not responsible for your success directly but you may look to them for strength and guidance at times when you are unsure. However, it is still your dream no matter what. Sometimes when we don't have that encouraging warm and fuzzy relationship, or if we have formed some kind of dependency on someone else, they can become a crutch and a "reason" why you have not gotten as far as you wanted to. Dating/being married to someone who interferes with your vision, breaks down your self-esteem and demand you to change your focus will make you want to give up. When you are given an ultimatum to choose between your relationship or your dreams, you have to determine which is more important to you. You may need to implement compromise but at the end of the day your mate should support what you want in life.

We all want to have a positive and healthy loving relationship with someone who is kind, respectful and a cheerleader for our dreams. However, we must first engage in that kind of relationship with ourselves and provide our own encouragement. If your mate is not motivating you to your highest self, what are your choices? Do you stay? Do you adapt to an environment that you don't want to live in or do you assert yourself and tell them what you need to feel loved? Relationships are give and take and you may have to show your loved one how it's done, by how you treat yourself. You may find that they just don't know what or how to support you. How you wish to be perceived should mirror what's in your mind, soul and spirit. How can you request treatment that you don't exemplify or reciprocate?

What do you want/need from your mate? (Or potential mate)

_____
_____
_____
_____
_____
_____
_____

How do you support your mate's passion?

_____
_____
_____
_____
_____
_____

Knowing your needs and your mate's needs will create the blueprint on how to treat and **respect** each other.

Respect is defined as, "a feeling of deep admiration for someone or something elicited by their abilities, qualities, or achievements." Respect is necessary when it comes to loving, learning and embracing the person you are and who you are destined to be. But before you seek respect, you need to respect yourself.

I deserve to be respected because

_____
_____
_____
_____
_____
_____
_____

You deserve every ounce of happiness. When you embrace the concept of respect within your relationships you will experience a great level of enjoyment. Iyanla Vanzant is known for saying, "Everything that happens to you is a reflection of what you believe about yourself. We cannot outperform our level of self-esteem. We cannot draw to ourselves more than we think we are worth." In other words, people will see your reflection and treat you accordingly.

Remember you create the kind of relationship you desire, by first having it with yourself.

Failures

When I think about everything I have accomplished in life, I smile at the successes and also cringe at how I failed miserably. I often viewed my failures as God telling me to give up because I did not understand how living for my calling could cost me my livelihood. I sacrificed my health and my safety; I compromised almost everything to pursue my passion because I believed I had a gift. Every industry I attempted to enter into I failed. However, I failed my way to success. Even though I did not sell out every theatrical production I produced nor have I made the NY Times Best Sellers List yet; I created networks, obtained new opportunities and built a customer base that is anxiously awaiting the release of *this* book. So even in my worst situation, my failures allowed me to walk through doors that were once locked.

When you are faced with failure, I challenge you to find the opportunities and possibilities that lie within. Think about what life would have been like for me if hadn't tried my chance at success after failure. Trying is the only way to win otherwise you never know. We all dream of being something greater in life, but so often we are fearful of failing. However, failure is the universal event that tests your commitment to what you desire. Failure gave me the "eye of the tiger" and the determination to come back bigger and better. I beat myself up for investing my entire paycheck when it came to financing my dreams because I believed that one day my dreams would provide another source of stable income for my boys and me. However, it took for me to hit rock bottom and almost lose hope of ever achieving success from my projects; the bottom is a place that I never want to see again.

I wasn't always this understanding when it came to failing. For me, it meant that I was not prepared for the journey ahead; therefore, I had to quit. Quitting before things got rough was my way of protecting my name, dignity and the money I had left. Even though we all handle failure differently, it affects us all in the same way. Before my mental transformation, failure made me reluctant to try anything and caused me to sabotage my mindset. Failure lowered my self-esteem. Out of fear, I convinced myself that I was not going to achieve anything - so pursuing it would be a waste of time. I fed myself those lies until it became a part of my mindset. I allowed fear to hinder my purpose and I gave it permission to alter my direction; headed somewhere I did not really want to go. Instead of writing, I found peace in helping others achieve *their* dreams because to me I had nothing to lose. How could I fail helping someone else? I was failing myself out of my own ambition and my own experiences. This behavior not only affected who I was but it also prevented me from becoming *who I knew* I was supposed to be. Now I want you to look at your life and see how failure affected you.

What did it stop you from pursuing?

1. _____
   _____
2. _____
   _____
3. _____
   _____

Even though we all have allowed the fear of failure to dictate our moves at some point in life; this fear is actually a positive thing. Being fearful of anything can provide you the extra will-power, assertiveness and determination to try harder to win the battle at hand. Just think, if you defeated every obstacle, obtained every dream or became successful with no opposition would you learn to struggle – because it will come. There is a saying, "To whom much is given, much is required" and that's where failure promotes progress. Failure is inevitable. It's going to happen, but the way you bounce back from it dictates whether you got the lessons. Failure will almost always explain what you did wrong and what you need help with the second time around. For example, when I co-produced my first stage play "Living your Life," I just knew I was going to sell out every show. I assumed that all of my friends, family, sorority sisters, masonic members, church friends and co-workers were going to purchase every ticket I had. So I decided not to promote that much because between all of the organizations I belonged to ticket sales would be covered. Was I ever so wrong! Even though I had a great turnout, I did not sell nearly as much as I assumed. So to me I failed myself and my cast because if I had of promoted the play properly, they would have performed to sold out audiences every night. Afterwards, I told myself I was never going to produce or write another play again, but 2 weeks later I was invited to perform that same play in Washington D.C. the next summer. So what do you think I did? That's right, I took my production down to Washington D.C., but this time around I promoted and received the support I knew the play deserved. However, if I had of followed my first mind and quit, I probably would not be where I am today. Instead of allowing failure to stop me, I gave it permission to teach me how to be better.

Looking back at your own personal or professional failures, I want you recognize the lessons you've learned and list them.

1. _____
   _____
   _____
   _____
2. _____
   _____
   _____
   _____
3. _____
   _____
   _____
   _____
4. _____
   _____
   _____
   _____

Now that those failures are behind us, how are we going to view failure moving forward? Remember failure is inevitable, but there are ways you can overcome and prevent it from recurring. You should try not to make the same mistakes twice; if you do it's only because you failed to learn the lesson the last time. But in the meantime, follow these tips when faced with failure or trying to shake off the bitterness that it can bring.

- **Embrace your mistakes** - Successful people don't see failure as catastrophic, but see failure as a guide for what not to do with the next attempt
- **Ask for help** ~ It is impossible for you to know everything so make someone else feel good about

helping you and in the process advance toward your goal.

Transformation Zone ~ Dig Deeper

Write down three ways you are going to birth positive relationships.

1. _____
   _____
2. _____
   _____
3. _____
   _____

Affirmation

I forgive those who have harmed me in the past and I peacefully detach from them.

Chapter 3
I Deserve Better

Coaching Corner

Before you embark on this chapter, ponder these questions and be prepared to answer them as you read each section.

Why do I need others to validate my life before I feel comfortable in it?
What opportunities did I miss because I was focused on someone else?

Cost Benefit

We all live with bruises and blemishes and we *do not* have to hide them. Life is full of obstacles and battles that may leave us bitter and injured. It is okay to hurt. It is even okay to be upset but is not okay to harbor anger and resentment. As I stated in the last chapter we may need to interact with others in some fashion to maneuver through life. When deciding who to allow in your "circle" you must examine a few items to ensure they will bring value and growth to your already momentous journey.

- *Are they knowledgeable and of the same caliber?*
- *Can they financially carry their own weight?*
- *Are they emotionally stable?*
- *What do they want and what can they offer?*
- *Do you have the time to invest in the relationship?*

You may read this list and immediately re-elevate your entire friend list and trust me, this is a good thing. Making sure that you align yourself with the right people is important. It is extremely difficult to deal with people who carry insecurities and a spirit of negative energy. These types of people are like parasites who enter your life to "take whatever they can" in order to breathe life back into theirs. To prevent this, my suggestion is that you thoroughly screen before you open up to people. Every person you meet does not deserve to have access to your life. They do not need access to your emotions, love or support. Some people can simply receive a "Good morning" smile or a "Have a great day" wave. When you let hurt people into your life, be prepared to be hurt. When you let drama in, be prepared to have foolishness surround you. Before you open up your life to others, make sure that their intentions will enhance your life and not slow down your progress.

My friend Vaughn once asked me, **"If the cost to you outweighs the benefit why do it?"** When he asked, I honestly didn't have an answer because I always saw myself as helping people instead of looking at any resources that I was losing. I always put myself last to guarantee everyone else's happiness. I reflected on Vaughn statement and I really had to ask myself was I compromising myself for others? Did they cost me more then they benefited me? What do you think? Answer the following questions:

What things or people in your life are costing you more than they benefit you?

_____

_____

_____

_____

_____

What purpose are they serving?

_____

_____

_____

_____

_____

Why are you still holding on?

_____

_____

_____

_____

_____

Do your answers put things into perspective for you? Now that you see how much you are investing freely, is there anything that needs to change? If you reconsider I challenge you to use this as motivation to start putting yourself first. I can't tell you how many times I have sat back and thought about all of the knowledge, money and time I gave to help others as I struggled to pay bills, keep food on the table and a roof over my head. It got to a point where helping depleted my finances leaving me "broke" *and* "broken". Now don't get me wrong, I don't regret helping anyone, but sometimes you have to know when to say "NO". There comes a time when you, the giver, must analyze how much of yourself you are giving and how it affects you if it's not being reciprocated. When the potential cost of something is greater than the benefit or the reward you should re-evaluate. Vaughn also gave me other suggestions relating to knowing who to fall back from. If you have friends in your circle that deplete you and/or try to deter you from your purpose, you must decide how to readjust the friendship or put an end to it all together. If you need help deciding, think about these additional points:

- *Is the relationship they seek, helping to get to where you want to go?*
- *If they are costing you happiness, why are you nurturing the connection?*
- *How will continuing this relationship, benefit you?*

I decided to invest more in myself and less into individuals who do not help my purpose to flourish. Have you ever heard of the cost benefit analysis? It is used to help you determine if the resources you put into something are greater than the return. If the cost is greater why invest? Make sense?

If having a passenger on board is costing you, have them get off at the next stop.

The Only Validation You Require Is Your Own

Why do people feel the need for others to validate *their* life before they feel comfortable living for themselves? It seems like validation is a requirement before people love, laugh and live life on purpose. Embracing the moves you make unapologetically will help to eliminate the idea of needing permission. Receiving suggestions from friends and family may be imperative when faced with a difficult situation or life-altering decisions; however, their words are *opinion* not law. Maintaining the power to make decisions for yourself should always remain your top priority. However, be cautious on who you seek guidance from and who you allow to coach you through life. To some people, validation implies control as you transfer to seeking answers.

The blueprint of your life was already written and the tools to progress in life are inside of you. I want you to look at all that you have endured. Next, focus on the lessons learned. Think about how you are using that knowledge to make your life better right now. Do you see how seeking validation is meaningless - you already know what to do. Some will never point you in the right direction of your destiny. They are too busy creating a path that will lengthen your travels out of spite, jealousy or revenge. Think about the time you sought guidance from someone regarding a situation that had you completely speechless yet had no idea what to do or how to bounce back. You went to someone hoping to receive concrete answers and solutions but instead you hear, "If I were you, I would… " After listening to *what they would* do, you realize that their answers do not match your personality. Do you really want to jeopardize your life finding peace the wrong way? Today, I challenge you to start taking your own advice. Who knows you better than you? Why do you think you had to go through hell, over mountains and through valleys before the blessings you sought flowed upon you? God will never put more on you than you can bear and every season you endured was preparation to receive and appreciate your deliverance. Your perseverance and determination during trials will provide the tools to lead you to the finish line.

Doing the work and digging deep is fundamental. The right answers are there. You will find them.

Some of you may say, "I have the lessons and know what I need to do but I am afraid of failure. This is why I seek permission or advice from others." I totally understand. I too am afraid of failure, but success is birthed from it. You must feel the pain of struggle to appreciate the joys of success. Let's imagine that after you finish reading this book you become so inspired and motivated to go after your dreams. You decide to go to your parents to ask their opinion and validation for your desire to quit your job, step out on faith and become a web designer. Not knowing how important this dream is to you they immediately tell you "NO" and suggest you play it safe with a local job. *They* think you should work your way up and see if you really want to change jobs. Do you see the potential dilemmas here?

Is this how validation often looks for you? Are you normally allowing yourself to be challenged to reconsider your purpose or passion after you discussing your ideas with others? If so, why do you continue to seek validation? Here is another example. You and your friend are going to New York to audition for a play on Broadway and while driving you ask for your friend's opinion regarding an opportunity you received in Los Angeles to star in a short film about "Anti-Bullying". Since she is eager to become an actress too (and somewhat silently jealous about the film), she tells you to hold off with accepting the role in LA until you see what Broadway decides. However, knowing that delaying your response to LA to wait for Broadway may cause you to lose the spot. You express concern to her feeling hopeful that she will encourage you to be a part of the film but instead she says, "Wait and see what Broadway says." However you know that delaying your response will make you lose that opportunity.

Seeking validation or permission may increase confusion and enable self-doubt. You must be willing to make some hard choices and firm decisions when taking chances. If you really need the advice of another I challenge you to seek wisdom from someone with formal knowledge and real experiences. Someone who can teach you about the journey will prepare you for what is ahead no matter which way you decide to go. In an effort to listen to my own voice and self-validate, I have started:

- *Leaning on myself, trusting and believing in my opinion and having faith in my vision.*
- *Before I call anyone to ask their opinion, I will first ask myself, "What do I hope that person tells me?" Then tell it to myself.*

Transformation Zone

Name three things that are costing you more than they are benefiting you.

1. _____
2. _____
3. _____

Affirmation

My ability to conquer my challenges is limitless; my potential to succeed is infinite.

Chapter 4
Love the Real You Purposely

Coaching Corner

Before you embark on this chapter, ponder these questions and be prepared to answer them as you read each section.

Am I so unhappy with myself that I allow others to redefine who I am?
What do I need to do to become more comfortable in my skin?
What would my life be like if I hadn't allowed people's suggestions to dictate my moves?
How can I say I love and respect myself when I give others the power to control my mindset?

Know your Worth

Malcolm X said it best, "We cannot think of being acceptable to others until we have first proven acceptable to ourselves." Knowing your self-worth is just as important as knowing your address and social security number. Your self-worth is what dictates how you treat yourself and how others should treat you. At the present time, how would you rate your self-worth on a scale of 1 to 10, with 1 being the lowest and 10 the highest? (Circle one)

1   2   3   4   5
6   7   8   9   10

Understanding your self-worth and believing it will help determine what you may need to adjust. If you circled any number less than 5, I want to help you raise that to a 10. I don't know what occurred in your life to make you feel this way but when we feel *less than great* about ourselves, people around us will treat us that way. It's time to do some soul-searching and painful digging to get to the root of the problem.

Who destroyed your self-esteem?

___

How old were you when it first occurred?

___

What transpired to make you feel this way?

___

What have you been doing to rebuild it?

___

Dealing with your past and adjusting your outlook is a step in the right direction. As I said earlier, carrying around baggage from your past continues to deprive you of what you are most deserving of – happiness right now! Let's work on rebuilding. You can make over your exterior by applying makeup, getting your hair done and dressing up in stylish clothes, but it's pretty difficult to do the same internally without pretending. How you feel on the inside is reflected through your demeanor, personality or behaviors and it's in those reflections where people learn how to handle you. When your opinion of yourself is high, then it is said that you hold high standards and you will accept nothing but the best and live a rewarding and purposeful life. However, if your opinion is low and your standards are relaxed, you can become a target for health issues, unhealthy relationships or abuse. Knowing your worth also refers to how you value your level of importance. You can't claim to love yourself but devalue yourself to gain attention and affection. Just like you can't brag about your accomplishments but deny yourself the rewards that follow?

Even in your weakest moments you can add value with your talents, personality or loving demeanor. Just because you failed in a particular area doesn't mean that you are a complete failure. Believe in yourself and know that in spite of all your mess you are still a 10. Your past has made you stronger and does not define you. Hopeful thoughts and subsequent actions can transform your life into something that most never dreamed about.

I was in a situation where my mindset was being controlled by guilt, blame and shame. My worth was being challenged because I was reminded of my past. Maybe you are experiencing this? Blame, shame and guilt are the 3 most effective ways to destroy your self-worth because they play on your sub-conscious. Until you disown the detrimental attitudes that you accept so freely, you will continue to rate yourself lower on the self-confidence scale. You can't control how people respond to you, but you can control how you respond to them. In an effort to remove your disparaging thoughts, we need to mentally and emotionally delete the baggage you have been carrying. Answer the questions below.

What has happened in my life that makes me feel guilty?

_____
_____
_____
_____
_____

What things have caused me to be angry and/or bitter?

1. _____
   _____
2. _____
   _____
3. _____
   _____
4. _____
   _____

What do I blame myself for daily?

_____
_____
_____

_____
_____
_____
_____

Am I shamed of who I am as a person? (Why)

_____
_____
_____
_____
_____
_____
_____

Allow the answers above to be food for thought. Use the ideas below to increase and maintain your self-worth.

- *Pray. Meditate. Be Still.*
- *Before falling asleep write down something you feel proud about.*
- *Don't accept anything that is not a reflection of your purpose.*
- *Tell yourself you are a good person.*
- *Say no! Learn the art of saying no without offending.*
- *Make mistakes and smile while learning the lesson.*
- *Speak up for yourself in every area of your life.*
- *Stay connected to what you want.*
- *Develop a relationship with money that allows you to live the way you want.*
- *Forgive yourself.*

Believing in what you want for yourself is the one of the biggest accomplishments that you will achieve right before you hit the mark of success. No matter what you encounter in life, there are two things for sure: **You** only get one chance at living a full life and **You** have to make the best of it. Stop discounting yourself because of your imperfections. Maintain your respect, increase your confidence and remember you are still worthy.

It's Time to Transform Your Mindset

Have you ever heard of the phrase, "Capturing a person's mind is the key to controlling their life"? When it comes to learning how to love and believe in yourself you must understand the power of your mind. A healthy and positive mindset is important to have to enjoy your success and handle your failures. This is also why it's extremely important who you allow in your personal space. If you are the type of person who is hard on yourself, downplay your strengths and persuade yourself to believe that you're less than - the last thing you need is someone who speaks with the same tongue. Romans 12:1-2 tells us that, "the way we are "transformed," the way we learn to live Christ's Life, is by the renewing of our minds". The power of change lies within the very thoughts you believe and nurture daily, whether subconsciously or on purpose.

You will find it difficult to receive love if you don't understand the love within. You will struggle to reach your final destination if you don't believe you are worth traveling past failures. What you get out of life is a direct reflection of what you put into yourself. The power of positivity is real. Positive thoughts can change your feelings. A great strategy for renewing your mind is found in Philippians 4:8-9. It contains 8 elements to focus on to transform our minds:

"Finally, brothers, whatever is **true**, whatever is **noble**, whatever is **right**, whatever is **pure**, whatever is **lovely**, whatever is **admirable**-if anything is excellent or praiseworthy-think about such things. Whatever you have **learned** or received or heard from me, or seen in me-put it into **practice**. And the God of peace will be with you."

These 8 elements provide positive filters to help you focus on all that is good surrounding you. The power of words and positive attitudes will change a day of pain into a day of praise and purpose. Now let's play a game, I am going to list a group of words and I would like for you to list the first feeling or emotion that comes to mind.

Love	Abuse
Selfish	**Can't**
Don't	**Won't**
Refuse	**Appreciate**
Respect	**Stupid**
Incompetent	**Lonely**

Some of these words we use daily when either talking about ourselves or expressing concern about something or someone. These words can be feelings that either promote growth or stagnate the potential in your life. For example, a word that we often say and embed into our vocabulary is "can't". Let's examine this word for a minute. By attaching this phrase to your thought process you can permanently embed in your mind the idea that you are not capable of doing anything worthwhile. Have you ever been faced with the opportunity to live in your purpose or your passion, but rejected the opportunity because you felt as though you couldn't make it. You have worked, prepared and saved for the opportunity, but as soon as it presents itself, your response is, "I can't". If so – there is some reprogramming that must take place. Most are afraid of failure but did you know that many are also afraid of success. Denying an opportunity that you have prayed and prepared for is counterproductive and a clear indicator of fear. This reaction clearly points out road blocks that must be removed in your heart and mind so that you can move closer to your purpose.

Think about this scenario and answer the below questions:

What has stopped you from pursuing your purpose or passion?

1. _____
2. _____
3. _____

Where could you be right now if you had of said yes to opportunities?

1. _____
2. _____
3. _____

How can you change "can't" to "can"?

1. _____
   _____

2. _____
   _____

3. _____
   _____

When you change your vocabulary from negative to positive, you will gain control over your thoughts and actions. Transform your mindset by replacing can't with CAN and incompetent with CAPABLE. Be cognizant of the words you attach to your thoughts because your experiences will become direct reflections of them.

Be Comfortable With Yourself

Loving yourself is the easiest way to find peace and comfort within. You will never grow purposefully being concerned, moved or bothered with the thoughts of others. My mother used to always tell me, "People are going to talk about you, give their opinions and try to change you to make you fit into a box, but remaining who you are will keep you grounded to your purpose." Remaining grounded without apologizing is rewarding, however, we all know that without high standards this process can be daunting. When people feel that you can be easily persuaded, they may attempt to implement their agenda in your life to keep you broken on their level. In order to conquer this, you must enjoy and love the person you see in the mirror; including all flaws, insecurities and uncertainty. In my previous years I was not comfortable in my own skin. I knew I was talented but I doubted my ability. I allowed what people thought and said about me to affect my level of comfort and peace. For years, I lived as a person who wasn't sure of her own direction. Always altering what was important to me so that I could provide comfort in the lives of others. I lost years living my life through others' filters; I was neither confident nor comfortable enough with myself to accomplish my own goals. I am an educated writer, I know the ins and outs of my industry and where I want to be. I have traveled to ATL, NY and LA to be among those who made it, but since I felt I was undeserving I still ignored the possibilities. I gave up on my knowledge, hustle and desire to be successful and as others' dreams came true I began to fall into a state of depression. I knew that if I could lead someone to their destiny there was absolutely no reason why I was struggling to provide for my own destiny. I began to understand that when you lack comfort, confidence and belief in your abilities, you give away your purpose-- for free. It was rewarding to see people achieve but it hurt just as much because I knew that it was me who gave them the tools to make it. This is when I was forced to make peace with my past so that I could live purposefully.

Deny the need to punish or beat yourself up when things go wrong. I often have people tell me that they are their worst critic and they are perfectionists and disappointment or rejection will cause them to abort any mission. I know it can be rough but you must understand that the rejection or delay you experience does not indicate that you're unworthy. Look at rejection as God's protection from disaster. When someone tells you "No", there are three reasons why:

> *1. You are not prepared for the task at hand.*
> *2. Your higher power knows that this is not associated to your purpose; receive it as a blessing or at least, try to respect it.*
> *3. No does not have to be absolute. No can mean "Not now".*

Instead of just hoping to make the situation possible, be open to the possibility of "not now". You may not want to keep "making the best of a situation" when you are unsure, unprepared and uncomfortable. When you love yourself, the fear of failure is a part of getting the desires of your heart. When someone says no – this is not a trigger to criticize your efforts. Just take the time to reevaluate situations when delays or road blocks are experienced. When you know "The Real You" you understand that all experiences are benefits that bring you closer to your higher self.

Here are some easy ways you can begin the process of welcoming certainty, peace and comfort into your spirit so that more positive than negative can manifest into your life:

- *Take care of your body.*
- *Promote and maintain a positive mindset.*
- *Celebrate a healthy spirit.*
- *Repeat kind and loving words.*
- *Give yourself a break from seriousness.*

Do you see the pattern in the process of maintaining peace? It all focuses on you replenishing who you are inside. It does not include taking care of others, hustling to make other people famous or worrying about how others may view you, but it requires you to build yourself up. Being comfortable is being at peace with you. It's just that simple.

Transformation Zone

What three ways can you take back your mind, body and spirit so you can live in your purpose?

1. _____
2. _____
3. _____

Affirmation

My thoughts are filled with positivity and my life is plentiful with prosperity.

Chapter 5
The Power in Finances

Coaching Corner

Before you embark on this chapter, ponder these questions and be prepared to answer them as you read each section.

Why am I so eager to make money?
Am I saving to prepare for my future or spending to enjoy today?
How am I going to start repairing my credit?
Who am I going to contact to seek an investment for my purpose?

Money Doesn't Make You - You Make Money

Repeat this affirmation after me:

Money does not define me.
Money does not dictate my worth.
Money does not complete me.

We live in a world where money has become more valuable than life. People are stealing, murdering, embezzling and destroying families just for financial gain. These folks feel that having money makes life easier and more enjoyable. First - let's get out of the habit of looking for things to happen easier. I have yet to receive anything easily, no matter how positive I viewed the situation. The same thing applies with money. Having money to survive is what jobs are created for, however to some, the love of money becomes greed. Does having money remove your hurt, confusion or heal the broken person you see in the mirror every day. Money may add a temporary Band-Aid by affording opportunities to do things to take your mind off of your inner woes but are the issues gone? No! Having money does not always transform your life into something better if you are not transformed inside. Can money buy you happiness? Can money buy you peace? Can money buy your personal and professional security? The answer is NO. Again, it may create a temporary space of happiness, but once it's gone, will your happiness remain? Probably not, that's why I can't stress enough the importance of loving the real you. Trying to cover up the scars with *things* will ultimately fill very few voids.

There is something about having money that makes people feel important and attractive. Having money, for some people, makes them immediately feel like they have arrived. Having money allows you to dine at the most expensive restaurants and travel to beautiful parts of the world. Money gives you permission to be free. The balancing act is learning how to enjoy your freedom while not allowing the money to define you. There are a lot of people in our society who feel that money separates them from others. Using your financial status to gloat on what others don't have will only come back to haunt you later. Remember, what you have today can always be lost tomorrow so before you go bragging about your net worth, make sure you know how to keep it. Once it's gone and you are forced to become a common man again the reminders of who you were and what you had will torment you forever.

Mismanaged money can destroy your credit, relationships and business. Being a millionaire today and a person struggling in poverty tomorrow is a bitter pill that no person wants swallow. Let's focus on credit score and relationships. Look at how money has affected your credit and relationships and list them below.

How has the absence/abundance of money affected your credit score?

1. _____
2. _____
3. _____
4. _____

How has money interfered with my relationships?

1. _____
2. _____
3. _____
4. _____

When we think of money we think of the tangible paper and coins we can carry in our wallets. But in today's society, credit is the way many use money. Credit cards are plastic loans from financial institutions to make purchases and pay bills. It's not grant money or money that doesn't have to repaid, it's a borrowing system that can drown you in debt, hardship or leave you filing bankruptcy. Having a credit card is the not green light for you to go crazy in Neiman Marcus. The general purpose of credit cards is to provide emergency funds when the unexpected happens, not to shop until you drop to keep up with the Joneses. Your desire to be "like" someone can ruin your credit and it will cost you the ability to purchase a home or a car when the time comes. Have you ever gone shopping and tried to get the store credit cards to receive the 15% off discount only to be told that, "they could not make a decision at this time" which politely means "You were denied". How does hearing that rejection affect you? Think about becoming a homeowner with money for your down payment and all you need now is to get pre-approved. So you go to a bank or credit union to speak with a mortgage consultant and she tells you that they could not approve you for a mortgage because your credit is in poor standing. Having to put your dreams on hold because of a financial mismanagement can cost you your pride, drive and motivation to try again. Now think about your purpose and passion, if you went to a bank right now to borrow money to fund your upfront capital would you be approved? Do you now understand the dilemma that money and credit can cause you when you are trying to transform into the better version of you? Where do you think you can go with bad credit? Being responsible with money in your meantime is essential to your success and makes getting there much easier. Loving yourself is also about being able to live without foreseeable hurdles. The fewer pitfalls you must encounter, the better the journey will be. You deserve it that way. Here are 5 ways you can increase your credit score:

- *Dispute errors on all three credit reports.*
- *Negotiate with creditors to establish lower monthly repayment options.*
- *Do not max out your credit cards.*

- *Pay your bills on time using auto payments through your bank.*
- *Become an authorized user on someone's account whose credit of better than yours.*

Let's have a candid conversation about money and relationships. A key to maintaining a respectful relationship is by respecting people's time, space and money. There is nothing worse than having a friend who counts your money, remembers your pay day and helps you spend your money because they are broke. Not respecting folk's money is the fastest way to lose them. In addition to that, the #1 cause of unhealthy relationships and divorce is mismanaged money matters. There is nothing more disrespectful in a relationship than to have someone blatantly break a promise regarding money. When you borrow money, you never know the inconvenience you are causing or the responsibilities your friend may be shifting to assist you. I have heard some people say as a rebuttal, "Don't borrow it if you can't afford to give it back" and that is correct. Some people will borrow money and never have the intentions on paying you back. No one wants to feel taken advantage of, so with the same respect with which they extended to loan it should be given back. When you don't respect financial help you burn bridges. Think about this, just say this is not your pay week, you come home to find that your electricity is off due to a power outage in the neighborhood causing you to lose all of your food. At that moment you realize you only have $5.75 in your wallet, $0.00 in your bank account, all of your credit cards are max'd out and you have four hungry children. You begin to panic. You pick up the phone to call your best friend to see if she can loan you some money, but then you remember that you never paid her back the $75.00 she loaned you 3 weeks ago. Then you call your mom to see if she will allow you to use her credit card to get food for the children, but she reminds you that you never paid the bill you created on her credit card 3 years ago. Now your children are crying and you have no one else you can call to help you. Even though this may be a bit extreme what would you do? Burning bridges and not paying back loans can backfire on you leaving you helpless. Every now and again we need to look to our friends for help regardless of the situation. But how do you expect for people to continue assisting you when you can't uphold your end of the deal or at least communicating that to the person you owe. A simple, "Hey, I know I said_____ but I will pay you back on_____ because _____ happened". This keeps the level of respect high and everyone on the same page. After digesting this, I want you to think about everyone you owe or how many bridges you burned by not remaining true to your word. If you had the opportunity to rebuild broken bridges burned by money issues could you love and respect yourself and that other person enough to face them today with the money you owe them in hand? If so, what's stopping you? Healing damaged relationships when it's comes to finances are easy when you:

- *Acknowledge you were wrong.*
- *Apologize for your actions and lack of communication.*
- *Accept their feelings.*
- *Arrange to make good on the situation that you abandoned.*

You should never allow money the power to destroy anything in your life. Relationships are vital to your success because you can't live in this world alone. So treat your relationships with the utmost respect, love and discernment. Money will come and go but true friendships are hard to come by. Here are 5 additional ways you can prevent money from negatively affecting your relationships.

- *Pay people back the money you owe them.*
- *Always find appreciative ways to return acts of kindness.*
- *No matter how much money you have, always treat people with respect and love.*
- *Do your best to keep your word when offering financial help.*
- *Be honest with your financial situation.*

Financing your Purpose

When you think about pursuing your passion or purpose, the first thing you have to consider is how you are going to fund it or who is going to invest. Living in your purpose can sometimes be costly and require you to find money to start the process. I have seen a lot of people decide not to pursue their dreams due to lack of finances. Whether we want to agree or not, money does make the world go round and it's required to do almost everything in life. This holds true with this book you are reading. Before you were able to purchase, I had to make an investment in order to pay for the expenses linked to taking my manuscript and transforming it into a substantial piece of literature. However, we know that in today's economy the average person; does not have $2,000 to $10,000 thousand dollars to invest in a business full of risk. People are looking for guarantees and the fastest way to make money without losing any of it.

Unfortunately, I don't know of any opportunities that give money freely without requiring you to do some kind of work. Obtaining finances to pursue or support your endeavors can be a daunting experience but it can also be a rewarding one if you practice patience, learn who the key financial players are and partner up with others who share like-minded goals. The same holds true when it comes to becoming a homeowner, buying a new car or get out of financial debt. Knowing who to go to for help will ease the fear and eliminate the desire to keep delaying your passion of being a singer because you can't afford to travel to perform. When you understand that you have options you hold the power.

In Forbes magazine, there was an article, written by Kerry Hannon that highlighted places to go to get funding for your business, purpose or passion.

Personal Savings
Friends and Family
Banks and Credit Unions
Angel investors &Venture Capital Firms
Economic Development Firms
Corporate Programs
Grants
Crowdfunding site (Gofundme, Indiego)

This list should give you hope and options when it comes time to find money to fund what you desire to do in life. Keep in mind that when accepting money from others we usually have to be deemed serious and financially stable to do the right the money you are lent. Therefore, some people may require you have an excellent credit history and a visual business plan outlining your vision, targets, budget and execution. Going to others is helpful when you don't have much money but remember that people and especially financial institutions, don't give without an established return; whether the return is a stake in your company or their money returned with interest. So before you begin to seek assistance, decide whether you are ready to borrow, share notoriety or whether you want to be the sole funder in the process. Many people decide to hustle, fundraise and/or network with like-minded people who can mentor them until they are able to pay their fee. Examine your options, weigh out the potential and ensure that you can align and maintain the love you have for your goals why pursing them.

Transformation Zone

Understanding the important of finances, how will you begin the journey to financial freedom?

_____
_____
_____
_____
_____
_____

Affirmation

Prosperity within me, prosperity around me; abundance within me, abundance around me.

Chapter 6

In the Midst of Living, Never Forget to Love Yourself

Coaching Corner

Before you embark on this chapter, ponder this statement and question and be prepared to reflect on them as you read each section.

Today is the day I am going to start loving me, again, unapologetically.
What are some of the ways that I am going to remain committed to the Real Me?

Moving Forward

As we get closer to the end of our journey together, I want you to start thinking about how you are going to move forward with your new mindset. I pray that this book made you think and helped you find some answers so that you can walk in your purpose. Knowing your divine assignment, learning how to love you unapologetically and understanding what's holding you back from achieving, are the gifts that I wanted to share through this book. It will be difficult to move forward in life confused about how to achieve financial freedom, emotional stability and freedom to explore your passions, without first realizing and forgiving yourself and your past. Today I challenge you to leave every negative situation, blame and failure in this book. After today, they no longer matter and should not resurface in your mindset, your destiny or through your words.

In order to love the real you, you must first renew your mind, body and spirit. Renewing who you are and accepting who you are destined to become will make living purposefully a rewarding lifestyle. Remember what believe is who you will become. Therefore, we must transform and enhance our vocabulary. Speaking life into your existence will provide you with the confidence, self-worth and respect needed to help you embrace everything positive. Lastly, we must understand the power of relationships, finances and walking in our purpose and how it affects our overall progress. As you move forward in this journey, you may need to network, finance your passion until investors seek you and accept your divine assignment without hesitation. This entire process is how you begin to clearly love the real you. Now I know you may ask, "Where do I start?" I have created a checklist for you to find the areas that require some work.

Go through the list and write yes or no next to each one.

- **Do you love yourself unconditionally?**

  _____

- **Are you living in your purpose?**

  _____

- **Do you have education or certifications other than high school?**

  _____

- **Do you feel the need to be perfect?**

  _____

- **Are you still holding grudges against people who wronged you?**

  _____

- Have you shared with your friends how much you appreciate them?

  ___

- Do you have at least 6 months of your living expenses in a saving account?

  ___

- Do you have a retirement fund (IRA, 401K)? If not, why?

  ___

- Are you investing in any stock options?

  ___

- Are you working to obtain a credit score of 620 or more?

  ___

- Do you owe anyone money that you haven't repaid?

  ___

I Finally Love Me!

___

Shanel Cooper Sykes wrote an affirmation that I repeat every day and it goes:

"I AM NOT MY MISTAKES. I AM NOT MY OLD HABITS. I AM NOT MY PAST. I AM A BEAUTIFUL REFLECTION OF GOD. I AM FORGIVEN. I AM LOVED. I AM FREE."

You are more than your circumstances and what people give you credit for, but no matter what they say, you have to know all of this for yourself. I want you to think about where you were mentally before you began reading this book and where you are now after reading, take a minute and answer these questions.

Are you going to change anything?

_____
_____
_____
_____
_____
_____

What did you learn?

_____
_____
_____
_____
_____
_____
_____

How would you rate your self-worth?
(1 being the lowest and 10 the highest)

1   2   3   4   5

6   7   8   9   10

What are some of the ways you are going to maintain your self-worth?

_____
_____
_____
_____
_____
_____
_____
_____

What are you going to do to fix your finances?

_____
_____
_____
_____
_____
_____
_____
_____
_____

Loving you and remaining "Real" with yourself will go far. You may lose some friends, family and possibly love along the way and that's okay, but you need to be who you are, for you. There is no more time for fitting in – it is time to live on purpose with passion. I want you to use your responses throughout this book and the above checklist to create your new process. The thing I love the most about life is that it gives you the ability to reinvent by respecting the lessons learned in order to help you get it right the next time around. Welcome to your next time around, are you ready?

You may be tempted to fall back into what *was* your reality and that's okay. Just don't get discouraged if you fall or have a setback. Your commitment is everything and as long as you do not remain stagnant. You will reap the benefits and come closer to your truest self. If you are not growing you are not living. I would like for you to write this final affirmation letter to your old self, apologizing to her/him for everything you went through. How do you plan to start a new life receiving what you deserve, desire and dreamed of?

Dear_____

_____
_____
_____
_____
_____
_____
_____
_____
_____
_____
_____
_____
_____
_____
_____
_____
_____

Always remember, if you don't love yourself, who will? Your life starts and ends with you. It's time to change your mindset and **LOVE THE REAL YOU**!

About the Author

Creativity is a craft Charron Monaye has been honing since the age of 12. This Philadelphia native is an accomplished playwright, songwriter and award-winning author who use her gift to uplift others and provide a solution to social woes.

Charron's work as an author and playwright takes social issues, such as anti-bullying, police brutality and father's rights, head on in unconventional ways using an 'Educate with Entertainment' approach. The proof is in her published books of poetry "My Side of the Story" and "Living Laughing and Loving My Way Through" promoting self-love, positive relationships and the power of healing. After her success with poetry, Charron took her writing to the stage in her first play "Living Your Life", with the hopes of reaching a larger audience. She went on to write four more stage plays; "Get Out Of Your Own Way," "Why Can't We Be Friends", "Pawns" & "Saving Our Sons".

Charron has received several acknowledgements and awards for her work. In 2013 she was an honoree at the Girls on Fire Awards in Cleveland, Ohio; receiving the "Presidential Award" and "Best Independent Author" award. In 2014, she won "Real Life Based Stage Play of the Year" for the production "Why Can't We Be Friends" at The DPI 3rd Annual Playwrights Awards in Queens, New York.

Charron Monaye is a proud mother of 2 sons, Christopher & Craig, who are the inspiration and motivation behind her drive to excellence. She has a B.A. in Political Science, Masters in Public Administration and a certificate in Paralegal Studies. She is a member of Zeta Phi Beta Sorority, Epsilon Rho Zeta Chapter & Order of Eastern Star, Ruth Chapter #66 (PHA~ PA) and The Visionaries Entrepreneur Network.

Email: charron.monaye@gmail.com

Website: www.penlegacy.com

For the past 5 years, Charron Monaye has been helping women all over the world improve, enhance and elevate their life through books and theater productions. From relationships to social issues from finding their passion to starting businesses, women of all ages are discovering their power, passion and capability to live the life of their dreams… simply by changing how they think about themselves.

From this moment forward, you have a new opportunity to begin again. This is your chance to live the purposeful life you desire.

Check out other books by the Author.

Learn more about Charron Monaye at website: www.penlegacy.com

Facebook: Pen Legacy ; Instagram: @ Mzmonaye ; Twitter: @PenLegacy

To Order Bulk Copies of Books by Charron Monaye

*Any orders of 15 copies or more, please email:
lovetherealyou0510@gmail.com
for discounted rates.*

Please leave a review of this book at
http://www.amazon.com/Love-The-Real-Charron-Monaye/dp/0996188002

www.ingramcontent.com/pod-product-compliance
Lightning Source LLC
Chambersburg PA
CBHW072100290426
44110CB00014B/1761